For Ajax Heos—B.H.

*Library of Congress Cataloging-in-Publication Data*
Names: Heos, Bridget, author. | Clark, David, 1960 March 19– illustrator.
Title: Just like us!, fish / by Bridget Heos ; illustrated by David Clark.
Other titles: Fish
Description: Boston ; New York : Houghton Mifflin Harcourt, [2018] | Audience: Ages 4–8. | Audience: K to grade 3.
Identifiers: LCCN 2016028102 | ISBN 9780544570955 (hardcover)
Subjects: LCSH: Fishes—Juvenile literature. | Fishes—Behavior—Juvenile literature.
Classification: LCC QL617.2 .H46 2018 | DDC 597—dc23 LC record available at https://lccn.loc.gov/2016028102

Manufactured in China
SCP 10 9 8 7 6 5 4 3 2 1
4500709325

| Lexile Level | Guided Reading | Fountas & Pinnell | Interest Level |
| --- | --- | --- | --- |
| 850 | P | P | K–3 |

# JUST LIKE US! FISH

by Bridget Heos

illustrated by David Clark

Peachtree

HOUGHTON MIFFLIN HARCOURT
Boston    New York

# FISH

## The Inside Scoop

**PEOPLE WALK ON LAND** and need air to breathe. Fish, on the other hand, have fins and spend their whole lives underwater. So how could we be anything alike? Well, did you know that fish can be doting parents and good teammates? Or that they go to the spa, where they are pampered by other fish? They also use weapons to hunt—and armor to protect themselves. Some fish even use lures to, well, go fishing! Read on to learn all about our awesome aquatic amigos!

# JUST KEEP SWIMMING, SWIMMING, SWIMMING

**PEOPLE NEED OXYGEN** to live. So do fish. But fish breathe with gills, not lungs. Oxygen from the water passes through the walls of the gills and into the fish's blood vessels, where it is carried throughout the body. When people exercise, they breathe harder. The athletes of the fish world are no different. Great white sharks can swim at speeds of 15 miles (24 kilometers) per hour—nearly three times as fast as an Olympic swimmer. To do this, they need lots of oxygen! So they have to swim day and night to keep oxygenated water streaming over their gills. In fact, if a great white shark stops swimming, it drowns. They don't just *like* to move it, move it—they have to!

# EVERY BREATH YOU TAKE

**JUST AS PEOPLE** need scuba gear to breathe underwater, fish need special equipment if they are to survive on land. The mudskipper spends up to 90 percent of its time on shore, crawling around on pectoral fins that resemble legs. But it doesn't have a tiny fish scuba mask. Instead, it fills pouches in its cheeks with water—the fish equivalent of an oxygen tank. The mudskipper's gills absorb oxygen from the water in the pouch. Fish out of water? Not the mudskipper, which runs, hops, and even climbs trees thanks to its constant oxygen supply!

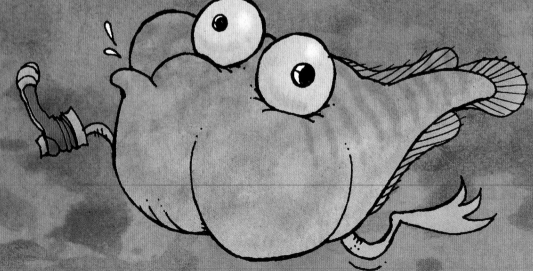

# LEAVE THE LIGHT ON

**UNLIKE MUDSKIPPERS**, most fish see no reason to leave the water. After all, there are plenty of fish in the sea! Some fish use tools to catch their prey—namely fishing rods! The deep-sea anglerfish has been fishing for much longer than humans have. It has a rod protruding from its forehead—an adapted dorsal fin. For a lure, the anglerfish uses a blob that glows in the dark because of bacteria living inside the fish. In the pitch darkness of the deep ocean, the lure attracts other fish. When they swim closer to investigate, the anglerfish eats them.

Only the female anglerfish goes fishing. The much smaller male just sinks his jaws into the female and feeds off her as a parasite. Over time, he loses his eyes and organs, and eventually he shares the female's skin and bloodstream. Talk about a close relationship. These fish are joined at the hip—and everywhere else!

**Red Light, Green Light** Fish were lighting up the night for millions of years before the invention of the lightbulb. The stoplight loosejaw has red and green lights behind its eyes. When prey swim over to see the light show, the predator grotesquely dislocates its jaw, and the bottom teeth sink into the prey. Then the stoplight loosejaw pulls its jaw back into its mouth—complete with the catch of the day. For this fish's prey, both red light and green light mean stop!

# RUMPLESTILTFISH

**PEOPLE USE STILTS** just for fun. But they're a matter of survival for the tripod fish. Food in the deep sea is scarce. Because fish in these parts don't get much to eat, they have to avoid swimming too much, which burns calories. The tripod fish has stiff rays at the end of its pelvic and tail fins, which act as stilts. The fish stands on the stilts, facing the current, and eats any fish that comes its way. It may be a bottom feeder, but thanks to its stilts, the tripod fish can still hold its head high.

# HOME SWEET TENTACLES

**AS YOU CAN SEE,** it's a fish eat fish world, and no animal is immune to attacks from larger—or more vicious—ones. So fish must also find means of protecting themselves. One way is by finding shelter. Little clownfish make their home inside a sea anemone. If a big, bad fish comes along, the anemone stings it. The clownfish is immune to the poisonous stings because it is covered with a layer of protective mucus.

**Roomies** Clownfish have several roommates. There is one female, which lays the eggs, one male, which fertilizes the eggs, and several other smaller males. If the female dies, her mate undergoes a sex change. The new female lays the eggs, and one of the other males becomes her mate.

ZAPP

# EXTRA CRUNCHY

**ARMOR IS ANOTHER FORM OF PROTECTION** used by humans and fish alike. The porcupine fish has a unique coat of armor covered in spines. Normally, these lay flat. But the fish can inflate itself with water—like a balloon—until the spines stand on end. In addition to being sharp, these spines contain poison, which deters most would-be predators. But some of the ocean's biggest and baddest—sharks, tuna, and marlins—still eat the fish, apparently enjoying their *poisson* with a side of poison.

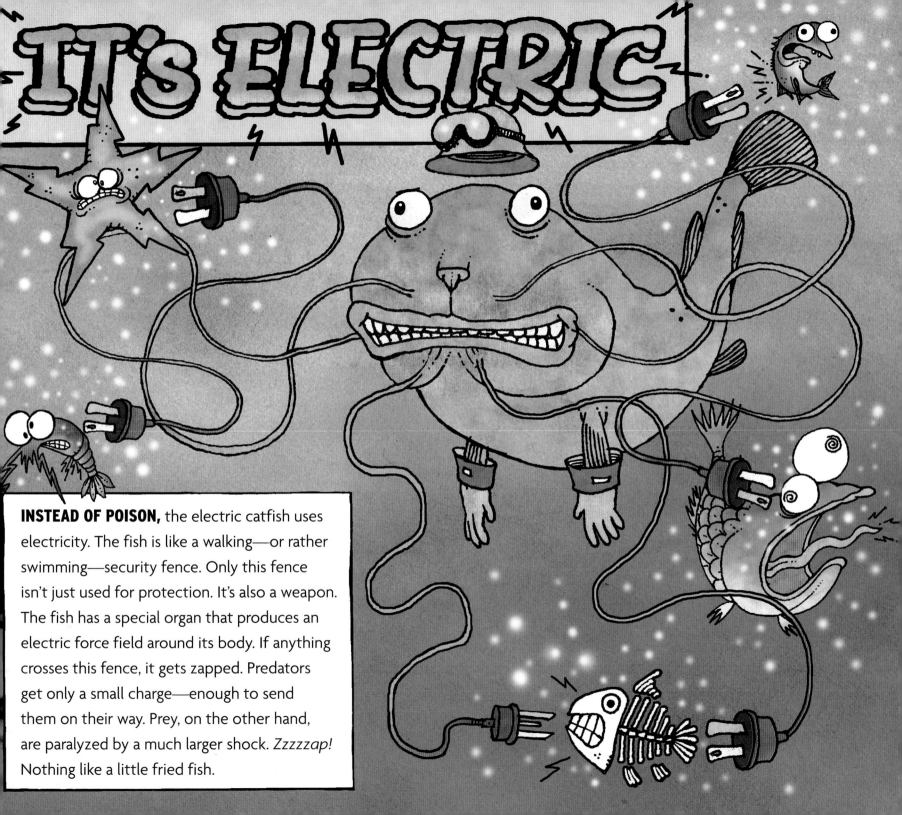

# IT'S ELECTRIC

**INSTEAD OF POISON,** the electric catfish uses electricity. The fish is like a walking—or rather swimming—security fence. Only this fence isn't just used for protection. It's also a weapon. The fish has a special organ that produces an electric force field around its body. If anything crosses this fence, it gets zapped. Predators get only a small charge—enough to send them on their way. Prey, on the other hand, are paralyzed by a much larger shock. *Zzzzzap!* Nothing like a little fried fish.

# GETTING SCHOOLED

**EVERYBODY KNOWS** there is safety in numbers. If danger arises, people in a community have each other's backs. So do fish! While some fish are solitary, others live in schools that can number in the millions. Schooling offers protection against larger fish in two ways. First, there are many eyes to watch for predators. If one anchovy senses trouble, it darts in the opposite direction, and the group follows suit. Second, it is difficult for a predator to focus on one fish among many. The hunter's eyes naturally wander from fish to fish, making it difficult to zero in on any one tasty morsel.

**En Garde!** Schooling isn't foolproof. For the marlin, a school of fish is an all-you-can-eat buffet. The marlin uses its sword-shaped snout to attack schools of fish that other predators ignore. The fastest animal in the ocean, it races over to a swirling swarm of tuna or mackerel and slashes its sword from side to side. Then it eats the injured and dead fish. Mmm . . . sushi. So delicious!

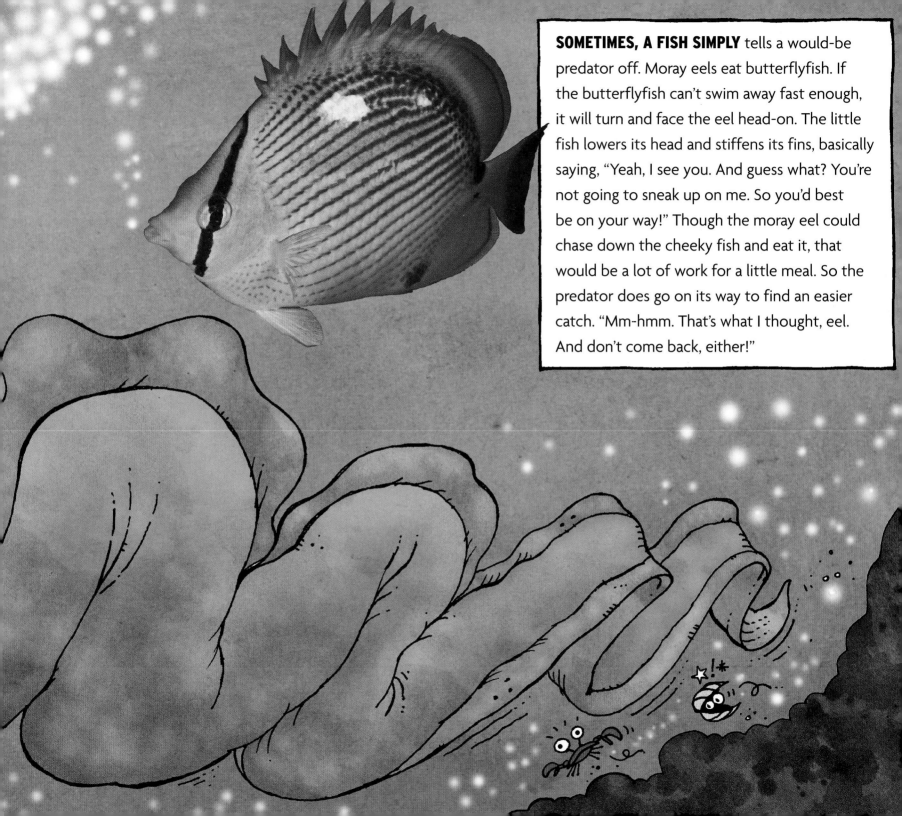

**SOMETIMES, A FISH SIMPLY** tells a would-be predator off. Moray eels eat butterflyfish. If the butterflyfish can't swim away fast enough, it will turn and face the eel head-on. The little fish lowers its head and stiffens its fins, basically saying, "Yeah, I see you. And guess what? You're not going to sneak up on me. So you'd best be on your way!" Though the moray eel could chase down the cheeky fish and eat it, that would be a lot of work for a little meal. So the predator does go on its way to find an easier catch. "Mm-hmm. That's what I thought, eel. And don't come back, either!"

# AHH... THE SPA

**CLEANER WRASSES HAVE A UNIQUE WAY** of avoiding being eaten. They pamper bigger fish! The brightly colored wrasses dance around to advertise their spa services, and a line forms. After all, even scary fish like barracudas crave some personal attention from time to time. Now, using their teeth as tweezers, the wrasses remove dead skin and parasites from the big fish. Ah, that's the stuff! In exchange, the big fish don't eat the little workers. On the contrary: they stay perfectly still for their beauty treatments.

Usually the cleaner wrasse is content to eat the exfoliated snacks from its customers. But sometimes, the little fish gets greedy and takes a bite out of a big fish's skin. The big fish doesn't retaliate. It simply swims away—offended, of course. The wrasse's coworker, on the other hand, will chase the biter, as if to say, "What are you doing? That was one of our best customers!"

# DRESSED TO IMPRESS

**WHEN THEY'VE EATEN THEIR FILL**—and avoided being eaten—fish turn their attention to romance. People dress to impress, and so do fish. A full 25 percent of all ocean species visit coral reefs to feed at some point. In this big-city atmosphere, a fish needs to stand out to find its special someone. Bright colors and bold patterns are the online dating of the fish world. These allow fish to find their match—fish of the same species with whom they can then spawn (which means the female lays eggs and the male fertilizes them).

# NO PLACE LIKE HOME FOR THE SPAWNING DAYS

**SALMON LIVE IN THE OPEN OCEAN,** but that's not where they spawn. They were hatched in a freshwater stream many miles away. Like people heading home for the holidays, salmon return home too. But it's far from a matter of hopping on a plane. First, the adult salmon swim to where the river meets the sea. Then they follow their sense of smell to their birthplace, up to 1,000 miles (1,609 kilometers) upstream. In the process, they swim against white-water currents and leap waterfalls up to 10 feet (3.5 meters) tall. When they finally reach their destination, the males and females spawn.

The baby salmon, or fry, are on their own as their exhausted parents slowly drift downstream. Their fat, silver bodies are now lean and greenish brown. Many are so exhausted that they don't even survive the passage back to the ocean. After all, the journey home may have been a trip, but it was no vacation!

**Even Fish Need Water Wings** With Mom and Dad away, the salmon fry will play. And for that they need water wings of sorts. The fish's heavy bones and muscles drag them to the bottom of the stream. That's good at first. It allows them to hide from predators among the gravelly riverbed. But when the salmon get a little older, it's time for them to explore. They swim to the surface and gulp the air. The air allows the salmon fry to float—not quite at the surface of the water, but somewhere in the middle. Now they can hunt and escape predators—good practice for their eventual lives at sea.

# LIKE PEANUT BUTTER AND JELLYFISH

**FISH PRODUCE MANY EGGS**—a female sunfish can lay 300 million in her lifetime! The eggs are scattered by the currents. Once hatched, the fish fry on are their own. However, some find babysitters—albeit strange ones. Young haddock and other species of fish fry swim alongside jellyfish. When a predator approaches, the young fish hide among the jellyfish's tentacles. Wanting to avoid being stung, predators stop short of the poisonous barrier. For some reason, the jellyfish don't hurt the little fish. The little guys may be immune to the poison. Or maybe the jellyfish actually like their little sidekicks.

# NUMBER 1 MOM & DAD

**WHILE MANY FISH PARENTS** leave their eggs behind and hope for the best, others care for their young like human mamas and daddies. The seahorse father keeps his babies in a sort of front pack. First he carries the eggs in the pouch. When they hatch, the babies are kept warm and snug inside the pouch too.

Cichlid parents, on the other hand, cradle their young in their mouths. Once hatched, the young leave the warmth of their parents' breath, but are still guarded closely. If the fry are scared, they'll dart back into a parent's mouth. Like moms and dads tucking their children in, cichlid parents scoop their young up into their mouths at nightfall, place them in a little pit in the ocean floor, and watch over them until morning. Rock-a-bye, fish fry, on the sea floor . . .

Protective parents, fierce hunters, and even beauty buffs, fish really are a lot like us. In fact, if people lived under the sea, we'd probably get along swimmingly with the fish. So cheers to you, our finned friends. If you ever see us swimming by, please be sure to wave!

# SAY WHAT?

**dorsal fin** a single fin on the back of a fish or whale.

**fertilize** to add male sperm to a female egg, resulting in a new organism.

**force field** a barrier created by an invisible force, such as electricity.

**fry** baby fish (*fry* is both the singular and plural form).

**gills** the organs that allow fish to breathe.

**immune** unaffected by a disease or poison.

**paralyze** to cause something to be unable to move.

**parasite** an organism that latches on to another organism and feeds on it.

*poisson* the French word for "fish."

**predator** an animal that hunts and eats other animals.

**prey** an animal that is hunted and eaten by another animal.

**school** a group of fish that swim in a coordinated way.

**solitary** living alone.

**spawn** the process in which a female fish lays eggs and a male fish fertilizes them.

**tentacle** a flexible, unjointed appendage.

# BIBLIOGRAPHY

## Books

Beer, Amy-Jane and Derek Hall. *The Illustrated World Encyclopedia of Marine Fish and Sea Creatures.* London: Anness Publishing, 2007.

Galan, Mark. *Underwater World.* Alexandria, VA: Time Life, 1992.

McMillan, Everly, and John A. Musick. *Oceans: Life in the Deep.* New York: Friedman/Fairfax, 1997.

Reebs, Stéphan. *Fish Behavior in the Aquarium and in the Wild.* Ithaca, NY: Cornell University Press, 2001.

Wade, Nicholas, editor. *The Science Times Book of Fish.* New York: Lyons Press, 1997.

Walker, Pam, and Elaine Wood. *The Continental Shelf.* New York: Facts on File, 2005.

## Web Articles

Baker, Amber, and Ashley Koser. "Diodon Hystrix." Animal Diversity Web. 2014. animaldiversity.org/accounts/Diodon_hystrix

Castro, Joseph. "Must Sharks Keep Swimming to Stay Alive?" *Live Science*. May 28, 2013. www.livescience.com/34777-sharks-keep-swimming-or-die.html

"Clown Anemonefish." National Geographic Animals. animals.nationalgeographic.com/animals/fish/clown-anemonefish

"For Comparison's Sake: Aroldis Chapman's Fastball." ESPN.com. espn.go.com/blog/sportscenter/post/_/id/77608/for-comparisons-sake-aroldis-chapmans-fastball

Gardiner, Nick. "Hippocampus erectus." Animal Diversity Web. 2001. animaldiversity.org/accounts/Hippocampus_erectus

"Great White Shark." National Geographic Animals. animals.nationalgeographic.com/animals/fish/great-white-shark

Lee, Jeff. "Amphiprion percola." Animal Diversity Web. 2003. animaldiversity.org/accounts/Amphiprion_percula

"Mudskipper." Aquarium of the Pacific. www.aquariumofpacific.org/onlinelearningcenter/species/mudskipper

Ng, Heok Hee. "Malapterurus electricus." Animal Diversity Web. 2000. animaldiversity.org/accounts/Malapterurus_electricus

Patton, Casey, and Cathy Bester. "Banded Butterflyfish." Florida Museum of Natural History. www.flmnh.ufl.edu/fish/gallery/descript/butterflybanded/butterflybanded1.html

"Questions and Answers About Salmon." USGS. 2013. wfrc.usgs.gov/outreach/salmon.html

"Shark Basics." Florida Museum of Natural History. www.flmnh.ufl.edu/fish/education/questions/basics.html

Tung, Luana. "Makaira Nigricans." Animal Diversity Web. 2003. animaldiversity.org/accounts/Makaira_nigricans

Yong, Ed. "Cleaner Fish Punish Cheats Who Offend Their Customers." National Geographic Phenomena. January 7, 2010. phenomena.nationalgeographic.com/2010/01/07/cleaner-fish-punish-cheats-who-offend-their-customers

**BRIDGET HEOS** is the author of more than sixty nonfiction titles for kids and teens, including *Shell, Beak, Tusk; Stronger Than Steel; It's Getting Hot in Here; I, Fly;* and *What to Expect When You're Expecting Larvae.* She's also the author of the picture books *Mustache Baby* and *Mustache Baby Meets His Match.* Bridget lives in Kansas City with her husband and four children, and you can learn more about her and her books at authorbridgetheos.com.

**DAVID CLARK** has illustrated numerous picture books, including *Pirate Bob, Fractions in Disguise,* and *The Mine-o-Saur.* He also co-created—and illustrates—the nationally syndicated comic strip *Barney & Clyde.* David lives in Virginia with his family, and you can learn more about his books and his comics at sites.google.com/site/davidclark1988.

Photo Credits: Carlos Estape: 27 • Jurgen Freund: 14, 19, 21 • Rodrigo Frisione: 17 • Dr. Dwayne Meadows, NOAA/NMFS/OPR: 4 • Alex Mustard: 6, 25, 28 • NOAA: 12 • Joel Penner: 13, 23 • Daniel Trim: 9 • Solvin Zankl: 10